Reproductive Rights

MAKING THE RIGHT CHOICES

A Young Woman's Guide
to Contemporary Issues™

Reproductive Rights

Making the Right Choices

JENNIFER BRINGLE

ROSEN
PUBLISHING®

New York

To the JDAD women, who continue to inspire me
with their intelligence and courage

Published in 2010 by The Rosen Publishing Group, Inc.
29 East 21st Street, New York, NY 10010

Library of Congress Cataloging-in-Publication Data

Bringle, Jennifer.
Reproductive rights: making the right choices / Jennifer Bringle.— 1st ed.
    p. cm.—(A young woman's guide to contemporary issues)
Includes bibliographical references and index.
ISBN 978-1-4358-3542-9 (library binding)
1. Reproductive rights—United States—History. 2. Pregnancy,
Unwanted—United States. 3. Birth control—United States.
4. Teenage mothers—United States. I. Title.
HQ766.5.U5B75 2009
362.19'88800973—dc22

                                                                2009013721

Manufactured in Malaysia
CPSIA Compliance Information: Batch #TW10YA: For Further Information contact Rosen Publishing, New York,
New York at 1-800-237-9932

Contents

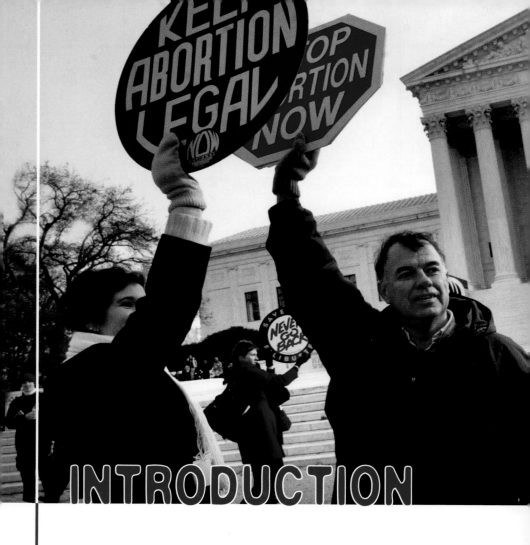

INTRODUCTION

Every spring and fall, antiabortion protesters begin their vigil. They make signs and posters, and stand in groups outside health clinics across the nation, voicing their dissent against abortion. The semiannual 40 Days for Life campaign follows the biblical belief that God uses forty-day periods to transform people, communities, and the world. For forty days, they protest. And for those forty days, Planned Parenthood's "Emily X" faces them.

She's the anonymous Planned Parenthood worker who chronicles these protests around the country. She visits clinics, blogs on her Web site, and raises money for Planned Parenthood through pledges, almost like a runner in a charity marathon. Her mission is to help women who feel intimidated by protesters and the message across that the right to choose is important and protected by law.

Both of these groups, the protesters and the people Emily X represents, are symbols of one of the most controversial issues in America: reproductive rights. Reproductive rights is a complex issue that involves not only abortion rights but also access to birth control, health care, and sex education. At the heart of the issue is the basic right of women to make choices about their bodies and control what happens to them—without the interference of the government.

For every single woman, no matter her age, race, class, religion, or political beliefs, reproductive rights is an issue that is crucial. Women all over the world deserve the right to control their own bodies. In addition, they all have the freedom to decide whether they are pro-choice or pro-life. As a young woman, your place in the fight is particularly important. You represent both the future of women's rights and the future of reproductive rights. The more informed and educated you become on the issue, your body, and your choices, the better equipped you will be to make the decisions that are the best for you.

CHAPTER 1

Sex: Choices and Consequences

Let's face it: teens are under a lot of pressure. You get pressure from school, home, and even your friends. A lot of things are expected of you, and sometimes, it can be a little overwhelming. For many teens, there's one type of pressure that can lead you to make what could eventually be a life-or-death decision—whether or not to have sex. The decision to become sexually active extends much further than the act of losing your virginity. With sex comes a variety of things, both emotional and physical, to take into consideration. How will you feel once you do it? Is your potential partner someone you trust? Are you in a solid relationship based on mutual respect and love? How do you protect yourself from pregnancy and disease? These are questions to consider before making your choice. And before you decide whether or not to have sex, you need to be informed about the consequences and how to make your experience a safe one.

MAKING THE CHOICE TO BECOME SEXUALLY ACTIVE MEANS MAKING BIG DECISIONS ABOUT BIRTH CONTROL AND DISCUSSING YOUR OPTIONS WITH YOUR PARTNER.

Many people have fought long and hard to ensure that the women of today have the right to do as they wish with their bodies. One major aspect of that is the right to use birth control. Birth control wasn't always available. For many women of the past, the options were unreliable at best and unhealthy at worst. Women today are fortunate to have many different options when it comes to birth control.

And if you're planning on having sex, it's essential that you practice safe sex by using some method of birth control. Birth control does much more than prevent pregnancy. It can save your life.

Since there are so many methods of birth control, it's important to know the facts about each one so you can decide which is right for you. Remember that many birth control methods have side effects that could be life-threatening. And none of them are 100 percent infallible. So it is always best to see a doctor and make an informed decision before engaging in sexual activity.

BARRIER BIRTH CONTROL METHODS

Barrier birth control methods physically or chemically prevent sperm from entering the uterus. Of all the barrier

CONDOMS ARE ONE OF THE EASIEST AND MOST POPULAR METHODS OF BIRTH CONTROL TO USE. SEVERAL ORGANIZATIONS, SUCH AS PLANNED PARENTHOOD, GIVE CONDOMS AWAY.

methods, only the male and female condoms help prevent sexually transmitted diseases (STDs) or sexually transmitted infections (STIs).

CONDOMS

One of the most commonly used forms of birth control is the latex condom. The condom is a latex or plastic sheath worn over the penis during sex. Condoms prevent pregnancy by capturing sperm and preventing it from entering the vagina. And because condoms prevent the passage of body fluids during sex, they also help prevent STDs. According to Planned Parenthood, the way a woman's internal sex organs are shaped makes women ten to twenty times more likely than men to get sexually transmitted infections. The cervix in teens and young women is especially vulnerable to infection. So it's essential that if you're sexually active, you use a condom every single time you have sex.

Condoms are highly effective, with only two in one hundred women getting pregnant when using them correctly. Many people use condoms because they have little to no side effects. Some people who are allergic to latex may not be able to use some condoms, but there are varieties made of plastic that they can use without irritation. Because condoms are inexpensive and widely available, they are an easy option for birth control.

To increase the effectiveness of a condom, you can use it in combination with a spermicide. Spermicide contains chemicals that cause sperm to stop moving, thereby preventing them from entering the uterus.

FEMALE CONDOM

The female condom is made from plastic and is used to prevent pregnancy and STDs. It's a pouch that's inserted inside the vagina. It has flexible rings on each end, and when inserted into the vagina, the ring on the closed end holds it in place. When the female condom is used correctly all the time, five in one hundred women get pregnant. And when they don't always use it correctly, twenty-one in one hundred women get pregnant. Using spermicide increases the female condom's effectiveness.

BIRTH CONTROL SPONGE (TODAY SPONGE)

One of the less frequently used methods of birth control is the sponge. The sponge is a soft, round piece of foam that contains spermicide and is about 2 inches (5 centimeters) in diameter. The sponge covers the cervix, preventing sperm from entering the uterus. The spermicide contained in the sponge also keeps sperm from moving.

Some women prefer the sponge because it doesn't contain hormones, and it can be worn for up to thirty hours. Others don't like it because it can be tricky to insert and remove, and it can cause vaginal irritation.

CERVICAL CAP

Another method of birth control that involves covering the cervix is the cervical cap. The cap is a silicone piece shaped like a sailor's hat that fits over the cervix. It prevents pregnancy by keeping sperm from reaching the egg. The cervical cap works best when used with spermicidal jelly.

Like the sponge, many women prefer the cervical cap because it doesn't use hormones to prevent pregnancy like some other forms of birth control. It can also be worn for up to six hours, so it can be inserted well before sexual activity. But for those who are uncomfortable inserting something into their vagina, the cap may not be a good choice.

CERVICAL CAPS ARE SMALL, RUBBER, CUP-SHAPED DEVICES THAT FIT OVER A WOMAN'S CERVIX TO PREVENT PREGNANCY. LIKE THE CERVICAL CAP, DIAPHRAGMS ARE SMALL, LATEX DEVICES DESIGNED TO COVER THE CERVIX TO PREVENT PREGNANCY AND DISEASE.

DIAPHRAGM

Like the cervical cap and the sponge, the diaphragm covers the cervix to prevent pregnancy. Diaphragms are shallow, dome-shaped cups made of latex. When used with spermicide, the diaphragm prevents pregnancy by blocking sperm and keeping it from moving.

Diaphragms are sometimes used by women who don't want to use hormonal birth control. But they can come out of place during sex, and they cannot be used during menstruation.

HORMONAL BIRTH CONTROL METHODS

Hormonal birth control methods release a hormone or combination of hormones into the body, preventing pregnancy. Hormonal birth control can be used with a barrier method for more effective results. It is very important to remember that hormonal birth control methods do not prevent STDs and that these methods can come with a variety of side effects.

BIRTH CONTROL PILL

One of the most common hormonal birth control methods is the pill. There are two different types of pill: the combination pill, which uses two hormones, progestin and estrogen, and the single hormone pill, which just uses progestin. Most women take combination pills. The hormones work to prevent ovulation, thus preventing pregnancy. The hormones in the pill also prevent pregnancy by thickening a woman's cervical mucus. This mucus blocks sperm and keeps it from joining with an egg. Birth control pills are only effective when they are taken every day, but even then they are not foolproof.

BIRTH CONTROL PATCH

You've likely heard about the birth control patch but wondered how it works. It seems unlikely that a patch

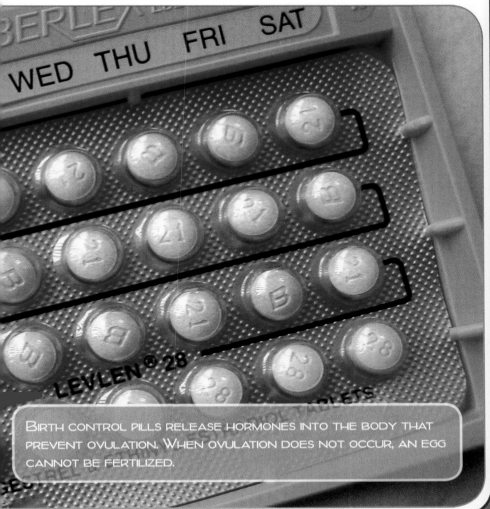

BIRTH CONTROL PILLS RELEASE HORMONES INTO THE BODY THAT PREVENT OVULATION. WHEN OVULATION DOES NOT OCCUR, AN EGG CANNOT BE FERTILIZED.

affixed to your skin would stay in place, much less prevent pregnancy. But that's exactly what it does. The patch is thin, beige, and has an adhesive side that sticks to your skin. Once attached to the skin, it releases the hormones progestin and estrogen into the system through the skin, preventing ovulation. The patch is worn for three weeks

AS THIS ROADSIDE SIGN POINTS OUT, ABSTINENCE IS THE ONLY FOOLPROOF METHOD OF BIRTH CONTROL. THE DECISION TO HAVE SEX IS AN IMPORTANT ONE.

2.5 Years of diapers = $2,327.00 And that's just diaper Sex can wait.

Made possible by the Iowa Dept. of Public Health & the Dept. of Health & Human Services

and is then removed for a week, which is usually when your period will come.

BIRTH CONTROL VAGINAL RING (NUVARING)

The vaginal ring is a small, flexible ring that is inserted into the vagina once a month to prevent pregnancy. It's left in

place for three weeks and taken out for the remaining week each month. The ring releases hormones (progestin and estrogen) to stop ovulation, preventing pregnancy. The hormones in the ring also prevent pregnancy by thickening a woman's cervical mucus. This mucus blocks sperm and keeps it from joining with an egg.

BIRTH CONTROL SHOT

If you're not afraid of needles, the birth control shot might just be the method that's best for you. The shot is an injection of the hormone progestin that prevents pregnancy for three months. Like other hormonal methods of birth control, the shot stops ovulation, preventing pregnancy. As with the pill, the hormones in the shot also prevent pregnancy by thickening a woman's cervical mucus. This mucus blocks sperm and keeps it from joining with an egg. The shot is popular with a lot of women, especially those who cannot take estrogen-based birth control medications.

IUDs AND IMPLANTS

An IUD (intrauterine device) is a small, T-shaped piece of flexible plastic inserted into the uterus to prevent pregnancy. Some IUDs work by releasing the hormone progestin to prevent ovulation, thus preventing pregnancy. IUDs are one of the most effective forms of birth control, with less than one in one hundred women getting pregnant while using them. IUDs are inserted by a health care professional and removed the same way.

Another method of birth control is the Implanon implant. It's a thin, flexible plastic implant about the size of a matchstick. Inserted under the skin of the upper arm, it protects against pregnancy for up to three years. Like some other methods of birth control, the implant releases a hormone, progestin, into the body. This hormone keeps women's ovaries from releasing an egg (ovulating), therefore, preventing pregnancy.

EMERGENCY CONTRACEPTION

Emergency contraception, also commonly known as the "morning after pill" or the brand name Plan B, is a set of pills you can take up to five days after having sex that will prevent pregnancy.

Emergency contraception works by releasing hormones into the body, just like the birth control pill does. These hormones stop the egg from releasing into the uterus, preventing pregnancy. A popular misconception about emergency contraception is that it basically performs an abortion. This is not true. Emergency contraception is nearly identical to a birth control pill, only it's taken after sex.

OTHER BIRTH CONTROL METHODS

Beyond the use of a hormonal or barrier method, there are ways that people have been preventing pregnancy for centuries. However, it is good to remember that, with the exception of abstinence, none of these methods prevent sexually transmitted disease.

WITHDRAWAL

One of the oldest methods of birth control is the withdrawal method. Basically, it involves the man withdrawing his penis from the vagina before ejaculation. For those who are good at knowing when ejaculation will occur, this method is fairly effective, with four in one hundred women getting pregnant if it's always done correctly. The only problem with that is it's often not done correctly, and the rate of pregnancy increases to twenty-seven in one hundred. But even when it's performed correctly, women can get pregnant due to sperm in pre-ejaculate (fluid that comes from the penis prior to ejaculation).

STERILIZATION

For those looking for a more permanent form of birth control, sterilization may be the best choice. It is almost 100 percent effective, preventing the release of eggs to the uterus by blocking their path in the fallopian tubes. This can be done a number of ways: tying and cutting the tubes; sealing them with an electrical current; closing with clamps, clips or rings; or inserting metal coils into the tubes. All of these procedures must be performed by a medical professional.

FERTILITY AWARENESS METHODS

Fertility awareness methods involve tracking one's ovulation in order to prevent pregnancy. Women using this method abstain from sex during their fertile period (ovulation), which usually occurs around eight days after menstruation.

While this method can work for some, it's still risky, especially if you're not totally committed to it. It requires consistency from both partners and careful monitoring of your body every single month.

ABSTINENCE

The only 100 percent guaranteed way to prevent sexually transmitted diseases and pregnancy is abstinence, or refraining from any type of sexual activity.

People engage in abstinence for a variety of reasons, aside from the prevention of pregnancy and STDs. Some of these reasons include:

- Waiting until ready for a sexual relationship
- Waiting for the right person
- Having fun with and getting to know a romantic partner on levels other than the physical
- Focusing on school, career, or extracurricular activities
- Staying in line with moral and religious beliefs
- Getting over a breakup
- Healing from a medical problem

There's another big benefit for young women who abstain. According to Planned Parenthood, women who abstain from sex until their twenties are less likely to get STDs, and in turn, they're less likely to become infertile or develop cervical cancer.

STDs: THE BASICS

Pregnancy isn't the only thing to consider when having sex. Sexually transmitted diseases or infections are also a risk of sexual activity. Even using contraceptives, there's no

100 percent guarantee that you won't contract an STD. When you think about becoming sexually active, it's important to know about these diseases and their symptoms.

HIV/AIDS

One of the most common, and certainly the deadliest, STD is HIV/AIDS. Human immunodeficiency virus (HIV) causes acquired immunodeficiency syndrome (AIDS). According to

Because HIV often doesn't exhibit symptoms, sexually active people should be tested for the disease. Many public health groups offer free or low-cost testing, such as that pictured here.

Planned Parenthood, there are 980,000 cases of AIDS reported to the U.S. government. About forty thousand men and women contract HIV each year. HIV is contracted through the mixing of body fluids during sexual intercourse, intravenous drug use, and transmission from mother to child during pregnancy, childbirth, or breast-feeding.

The symptoms of HIV include swollen glands in the throat, armpit, or groin; fever; headaches; fatigue; and muscle aches. Many times, the symptoms of HIV do not appear for at least ten years, making it easy not to know you have the disease. You can't know you have HIV unless you're tested for it.

Once HIV advances, it becomes full-blown AIDS. Symptoms of AIDS include:

- Thrush: a thick, whitish coating of the tongue or mouth that is caused by a yeast infection and is sometimes accompanied by a sore throat
- Severe or recurring vagina yeast infections
- Chronic pelvic inflammatory disease (PID)
- Severe and frequent infections
- Periods of extreme and unexplained tiredness that may be combined with headaches, light-headedness, and/or dizziness
- Quick loss of more than 10 pounds (4.5 kilograms) of weight that is not due to increased physical exercise or dieting
- Bruising more easily than normal
- Long periods of frequent diarrhea
- Frequent fevers and/or night sweats
- Swelling or hardening of the glands located in the throat, armpit, or groin
- Periods of persistent, deep, dry coughing
- Increasing shortness of breath
- The appearance of discolored or purplish growths on the skin or inside the mouth

- Unexplained bleeding from growths on the skin, from the mouth, nose, anus, or vagina, or from any opening in the body
- Frequent or unusual skin rashes
- Severe numbness or pain in the hands or feet, the loss of muscle control and reflex, paralysis, or loss of muscular strength
- Confusion, personality change, or decreased mental abilities

There is no cure for HIV/AIDS, but there are drug "cocktails" (mixes of different drugs) that can allow those with the disease to live for years. Continued research and new treatments may help people live even longer.

CHLAMYDIA

Chlamydia is like the stealthy ninja of STDs. It's the most common sexually transmitted disease. But because chlamydia often doesn't have any symptoms, many do not know they are infected. According to the Centers for Disease Control and Prevention (CDC), more than one million chlamydial infections were reported in the United States in 2007. This is why chlamydia is also one of the most underreported diseases. According to the U.S. National Health and Nutrition Examination Survey, more than two million U.S. residents between the ages of fourteen and thirty-nine are infected with the disease.

Caused by the *Chlamydia trachomatis* bacterium, the disease is especially dangerous because its symptoms are often very mild or absent. And usually when symptoms occur, they don't show up until one to three weeks after infection. In women, symptoms can range from abnormal vaginal discharge and pain during urination to fever and abdominal pain.

If left untreated, chlamydia can cause a variety of serious complications. In women, the infection can spread to the uterus and fallopian tubes, causing pelvic inflammatory disease (PID). PID can lead to permanent damage of the reproductive organs, causing chronic pelvic pain, infertility, and an increased risk of ectopic pregnancy (pregnancy outside the uterus).

Chlamydia is diagnosed through lab tests of urine or cervical specimens. Once diagnosed, it can easily be treated and cured with antibiotics.

HUMAN PAPILLOMAVIRUS

Genital human papillomavirus, or HPV, is the most common sexually transmitted infection. More than forty different types of HPV can infect the skin in and around the genitals and anus. HPV is not visible to the human eye, so many people with the STI have no idea they are infected. Most people with HPV don't develop symptoms. Sometimes, though, certain types of HPV can cause genital warts in men and women. The warts generally appear as small bumps or groups of bumps in the genital area. Their shape can vary: raised or flat, single or multiple, large or small, and sometimes cauliflower-shaped.

Other types of HPV can cause cervical cancer, as well as other less common cancers of the genitals. HPV can cause normal cells on infected skin or mucous membranes to become abnormal. The strains of HPV that cause warts are not the same as those that cause cancer. In 90 percent of cases, the body's immune system will clear the HPV infection within two years.

Genital HPV is passed on through genital contact, most commonly during vaginal and anal sex. A person who has been infected can unknowingly pass the disease on to others because he or she has no symptoms. According to the CDC, approximately twenty million Americans are currently infected with HPV. Another 6.2 million people become infected each year. At least 50 percent of sexually active men and women get HPV at some point in their lives. At any one time, about 1 percent of sexually active adults in the United States have genital warts.

As you may have seen in ads, there is now a vaccine to prevent females from the four types of HPV that most frequently cause cervical cancer and genital warts. The vaccine is recommended for those aged thirteen to twenty-six. There is currently no vaccine to prevent HPV in males.

HPV is generally diagnosed during a cervical cancer screening (a Pap test). There is no treatment for the virus itself, as a healthy immune system will usually fight the disease off on its own. In cases that cause genital warts, there are medications that can be applied to remove the warts.

HERPES

Herpes is another one of those tricky diseases with two different strains. Herpes simplex virus type 1 generally infects the lips and mouth, causing what is commonly known as fever blisters or cold sores. Herpes simplex virus type 2 usually causes genital herpes, a sometimes painful, incurable STD. The disease causes outbreaks of blisters on

SOME STRAINS OF HPV CAN CAUSE CERVICAL CANCER IN YOUNG WOMEN. BUT NOW THERE IS A VACCINE THAT PROTECTS AGAINST HPV, THUS HELPING PREVENT CERVICAL CANCER.

or around the genitals and rectum. These blisters break, leaving tender ulcers that usually take two to four weeks to heal. The first outbreak is usually the most severe, with milder outbreaks thereafter.

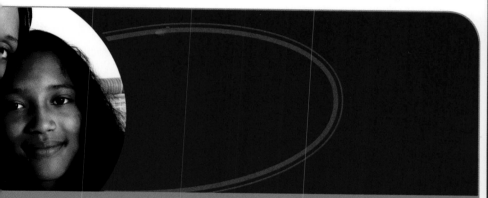

11 OR 12 YEARS OLD?

Now is the time to **protect her from cervical cancer.**

- Cervical cancer is caused by a common virus called the human papillomavirus (HPV).

- In 2007, about 11,000 women will be diagnosed with cervical cancer and about 3,600 women will die from it in the U.S.

- A vaccine to protect against HPV is now available. It can prevent most cervical cancers.

- Studies have shown the vaccine is safe and very effective.

- Doctors recommend the HPV vaccine for all 11 and 12 year old girls. If your teenage daughter missed getting the vaccine when she was 11 or 12, ask her doctor about getting it now.

According to the CDC, at least forty-five million people ages twelve and older, or one out of five adolescents and adults in the United States, are infected with genital herpes. Genital herpes simplex virus type 2 is more common in women than in men. According to the CDC, approximately one in four women are infected, while only one in eight men are infected. This may be partly due to male-to-female transmissions being more likely than female-to-male transmissions. So as a woman, you're far more likely to get this disease than your male counterparts. That makes it especially important to protect yourself from infection.

In order to protect yourself, you first need to know how the disease is transmitted. Generally, people get genital herpes during sexual contact with an infected person. It is important to know that you can get the disease whether or not the person has an outbreak. A person with no visible sores, who may not even know he or she has herpes, can pass it on to others. So just because things look OK doesn't mean they are.

The disease can also be transmitted by a person with herpes simplex virus type 1, which causes cold sores on the mouth. This occurs during oral-to-genital contact. But this type of infection is less common than the type 2 genital-to-genital infection.

There is only one sure-fire way to prevent herpes, and that's abstaining from sex. The next best method is engaging in sexual contact with one monogamous partner who's been tested for the disease. Latex condoms reduce the risk, but they do not always prevent the disease. People have gotten herpes while wearing a condom, so if you engage in risky sexual behavior, even with a condom, you are still at risk.

There is no cure for herpes. Antiviral medications can shorten and prevent outbreaks. Daily suppressive medicine can also help reduce the risk of transmitting to partners. But even with these medicines, there's no guarantee you won't have outbreaks or pass the disease to others.

GONORRHEA

Another of the more common STDs is gonorrhea. You may have also heard it called "the clap." According to CDC estimates, more than seven hundred thousand people in the United States get gonorrhea each year. But only about half of those infections are reported. This may be because, like chlamydia, gonorrhea is a virtually symptomless disease. Men may not have any symptoms at all, and if they do, they often don't appear until five to thirty days after infection. In women, the symptoms are usually very mild, if they appear at all. Symptoms in women include pain during urination, increased vaginal discharge, or bleeding between periods. These symptoms are often mistaken for other common diseases, such as bladder infections and yeast infections, because they have similar symptoms.

The disease can cause a variety of complications if left untreated. In women, it's a common cause of PID, which can cause chronic pelvic pain and even infertility. It can also spread to the blood or joints, causing a life-threatening condition.

Gonorrhea is spread through contact with the penis, vagina, mouth, or anus. Ejaculation does not have to

♀ THE CDC: KEEPING DISEASES UNDER CONTROL

The Centers for Disease Control and Prevention (CDC), located in Atlanta, Georgia, is part of the U.S. Department of Health and Human Services, which is the primary federal agency for conducting and supporting public health in the United States. The CDC's mission is to protect the health of all citizens through promotion, prevention, and preparedness. The organization conducts statistical and scientific research about a variety of diseases and health threats, trying to find ways to prevent, as well as cure, diseases.

Upon its start in 1946, the CDC's first goal was fighting malaria by killing mosquitoes. In the early days, the organization employed mostly entomologists (those who study insects) and engineers, not doctors. Once the fight against malaria and mosquitoes was essentially won, the CDC turned its efforts to preventing and eradicating other diseases.

Today, the CDC stands at the forefront of public health in its efforts to prevent and control infectious and chronic diseases, injuries, workplace hazards, disabilities, and environmental health threats. The organization conducts research and investigations in this effort, working with states and other partners to monitor and prevent disease outbreaks, implement disease prevention strategies, and maintain national health statistics. The CDC also guards against international disease transmission, with personnel stationed in more than twenty-five foreign countries. The CDC's Web site, www.cdc.gov, is a great resource for disease information, statistics, and guidance concerning diseases, including STDs.

THE CENTERS FOR DISEASE CONTROL AND PREVENTION (CDC) WORKS TO PREVENT AND EDUCATE THE PUBLIC ABOUT COMMUNICABLE DISEASES, SUCH AS STDS.

occur to spread the disease. It can also be spread from mothers to babies during birth. Like most STDs, the only guaranteed way to prevent it is abstinence. Condoms reduce the risk, as does having sex with one partner who has been tested. Gonorrhea can be cured with antibiotics.

According to the CDC, the highest reported rates of infections are among sexually active teens, young adults, and African Americans. This means you should be especially vigilant about keeping yourself safe if engaging in sexual activity because you're already more at risk just because of your age.

Syphilis

Syphilis is a bacterial infection that is passed through direct contact with sores on the infected person's body. Sores mainly occur on the genitals or anus, and transmission usually occurs during sexual contact. A pregnant woman can also pass it on to her unborn child.

Many people who get syphilis do not show any signs for years. Because of this, people can pass on the disease without knowing it. Once symptoms do occur, they come in three stages. The first, or primary stage, is usually marked by the appearance of a single sore. It's usually small and round, occurs at the point where the disease entered the body, and will heal without treatment in about three to six weeks. If left untreated, the disease moves onto the secondary stage. This is when skin rashes and mucous membrane lesions occur. The most common rash is rough, reddish brown spots on the palms or bottoms of the feet.

Other symptoms of this stage include fever, swollen lymph glands, hair loss, weight loss, headaches, and fatigue.

The late and latent stages can last for years if the disease is left untreated, and they can occur as long as ten to twenty years after infection. At this point, the disease can damage internal organs, including the brain, nerves, eyes, heart, blood vessels, liver, bones, and joints. Signs of this stage include lack of muscle coordination, paralysis, numbness, gradual blindness, and dementia. It can eventually lead to death.

In its early stages, syphilis is easily treated with an injection of penicillin. The disease can be prevented with the use of condoms, though abstinence is the only guaranteed method of prevention.

Trichomoniasis

According to the CDC, trichomoniasis is the most common curable STD in young, sexually active women. An estimated 7.4 million new cases occur each year among women and men. This means it's fairly likely you or someone you know has been or will be infected with this disease.

The disease is spread by direct genital contact. Most men don't have symptoms, but women generally do. Symptoms in women include a frothy, yellow-green vaginal discharge with a foul odor. It can also cause pain during urination or sexual intercourse, as well as irritation and itching in the genital area. In some cases, it also causes lower abdominal pain. Symptoms usually occur within five to twenty-eight days. The likelihood of a woman contracting

HIV increases if she's exposed to the virus while she has a trichomoniasis infection.

The disease is diagnosed through a lab test and is treated with prescription drugs, such as metronidazole or tinidazole, generally given by mouth. Using condoms helps prevent the disease.

BACTERIAL VAGINOSIS

One of the most common vaginal infections is bacterial vaginosis, or BV. With BV, an imbalance in the normal vaginal bacteria causes an infection. Signs of this infection include a white or grayish discharge, a bad odor, itching or burning around the outside of the vagina, and sometimes pain. But some women with BV experience no symptoms at all.

In most cases, there are no complications associated with BV. But the disease does have several serious risks. Having BV can increase a woman's chance of infection with HIV if she is exposed to it. It can also increase the chance that an HIV-infected woman will pass the disease on to her partner. BV is associated with a higher susceptibility to an infection that develops following surgical procedures, such as abortions and hysterectomies. If a woman is pregnant, having BV can increase the risk of some complications, such as preterm delivery.

While BV technically falls under the STD umbrella, the cause of the disease is not fully understood. Any woman, sexually active or not, can get BV. But sexual activity, particularly with a new partner or multiple partners, can increase the likelihood of getting the disease. Douching also increases the risk of getting BV.

BV is diagnosed through a lab test of vaginal fluid. While some BV infections clear up on their own, most need to be treated to avoid complications. Antibiotics, usually metronidazole and clindamycin, are used to treat BV.

LGV

Lymphogranuloma venereum, or LGV, might not sound all that familiar to you. That's because it's a less common disease in industrialized countries, such as the United States. But that doesn't mean you should think it can't happen to you.

LGV is characterized by raised bumps and/or ulcers on the genitals and swelling of lymph glands in the genital area. Symptoms of the disease are sometimes mistaken for syphilis or genital herpes. LGV is passed from person to person through direct contact with lesions, ulcers, or other areas where the bacteria lies. This usually occurs during sexual intercourse. It's treated with antibiotics, and condoms help reduce the risk of transmission but do not guarantee protection.

PELVIC INFLAMMATORY DISEASE

Pelvic inflammatory disease, or PID, is an infection of the uterus, fallopian tubes, and other reproductive organs. While it's not technically an STD, it is a common complication of untreated STDs, particularly chlamydia and gonorrhea. PID can damage the fallopian tubes, uterus, and ovaries, and it can cause infertility, ectopic pregnancy, abscesses, and chronic pelvic pain. According to the CDC, it's estimated that more than one million women experience an episode of acute PID. More than one hundred thousand women become infertile because of it.

The disease is caused by a bacteria associated with bacterial STDs. Women under the age of twenty-five are more likely to develop the disease than older women. This is partly because the cervix in teenage girls isn't fully matured, making it more susceptible to STD infection. The symptoms are usually nonexistent or mild, and include lower abdominal pain, unusual vaginal discharge, pain during urination, and irregular periods. PID can be treated with antibiotics.

Ten Great Questions
TO ASK A PLANNED PARENTHOOD HEALTH PROVIDER

1.
How do I protect myself against STDs?

2.
What's the most effective method of birth control?

3.
How can I get involved in protecting my reproductive rights?

4.
My boyfriend wants to have sex, but I'm not ready. How do I handle the situation?

5.
I'd like to get birth control, but I don't have insurance. What are my options?

6.
I'm afraid to talk to my parents about sex. How do I talk to them without getting embarrassed?

7.
If I can't talk to my parents about sex, who can I turn to?

8.
I'm afraid I might have a disease, but I'm not sure. What should I do?

9.
I'm pregnant and not ready to become a mother. What are my options?

10.
I've never had a gynecological exam. What can I expect?

CHAPTER 2

EXERCISING YOUR REPRODUCTIVE RIGHTS

Accidents happen. It's as simple as that. If you engage in certain types of sexual activity—even if you practice safe sex every time—you can become pregnant.

If you find out you're pregnant, you have several options. You can choose to have the baby and raise it, have the baby and place it for adoption, or end the pregnancy by having an abortion. If you decide to have the baby, there are several places to turn to for help outside of your relationship, family, and friends. Your local Planned Parenthood office has lots of information for pregnant women and new mothers. Planned Parenthood professionals can also help you weigh your options when deciding whether or not you want to have or keep your child. Other groups, such as Mothers & More,

offer support, advocacy, and education for mothers of all ages.

While outside sources like these are available, turning to your family, teachers, religious leader, or other adult you trust is always a good option when facing this situation. The guidance and help of adults you love and trust can help you as you make difficult decisions. They can help you with the responsibility of motherhood, should you decide to become a mother.

PLANNED PARENTHOOD HEALTH CENTERS ARE GREAT RESOURCES FOR INFORMATION AND GUIDANCE ABOUT SAFE SEX AND PREVENTION OF SEXUALLY TRANSMITTED DISEASES.

ARE YOU READY?

Becoming a mother can be one of the most exciting and special moments in a woman's life. It can also be one of the scariest. Even for the most prepared, motherhood can be one of the toughest challenges a woman faces. While it's rewarding, it's also a lot of work, and parents have to sacrifice a lot of time, money, and freedom to fulfill the responsibility of raising a child. Instead of hanging out with your friends, or spending your money on clothes and other fun things, your time and money will go to the care of your child. Before you even consider having a baby, you must consider the following things:

- **Time commitment** Children can put your school plans or a career on hold.
- **Energy and care** Children need parents who are loving, patient, and flexible.
- **Planning** Having children takes daily planning, as well as long-term planning for the next stages of the child's life.
- **Monetary commitment** Children need clothes, diapers, food, and health care, not to mention day care and other expenses.

In addition to these things, you must also think about how having a child will affect you physically and mentally. While it's amazing how our bodies can create a new life, it also takes a toll on you physically. Many women experience significant changes in how their body looks and feels, in addition to mental and emotional changes. Once you've made all these considerations, it's important to know some of the things to expect with pregnancy and motherhood.

PREPARING FOR MOTHERHOOD

Finding out you're pregnant and deciding to continue the pregnancy means you have to prepare physically and emotionally for carrying and giving birth to a child. Health-wise, this means you'll have to make some big changes to your usual routine in order to ensure your baby is as healthy as possible. Fortunately, prenatal care has come a long way in recent decades, and expectant mothers have a lot more knowledge and assistance in maintaining both their and their unborn child's health.

Women who are eighteen to thirty-five years old and healthy are generally considered to have a "low-risk" pregnancy. For those with a low-risk pregnancy, medical visits generally go on this schedule:

- Every four or six weeks, from the first to seventh month of pregnancy (the first twenty-eight weeks)
- Every two or three weeks in the eighth month (from week twenty-eight to thirty-six)
- Every week in the ninth month (from week thirty-six until delivery)

If you have a high-risk pregnancy, your health care provider may ask you to come in for prenatal care more often. During these visits, doctors will do a number of

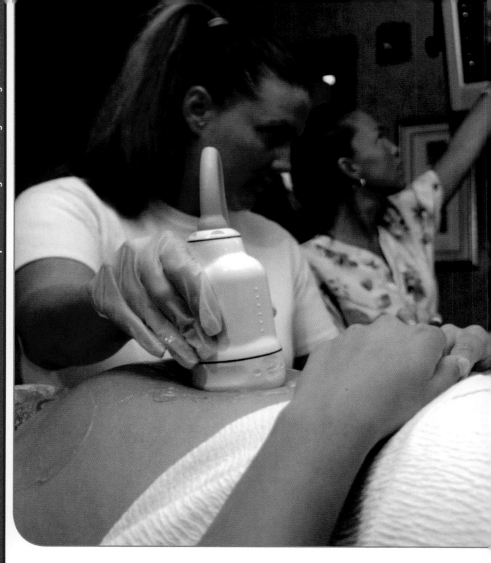

things. They include testing urine, checking blood pressure, checking weight, examining the abdomen to check the position of the fetus, measuring the growth of the uterus, listening for the sounds of the fetal heartbeat, and checking for swelling in the face, hands, or feet. During these visits, mothers usually have prenatal tests for birth defects. These tests include ultrasounds and amniocentesis.

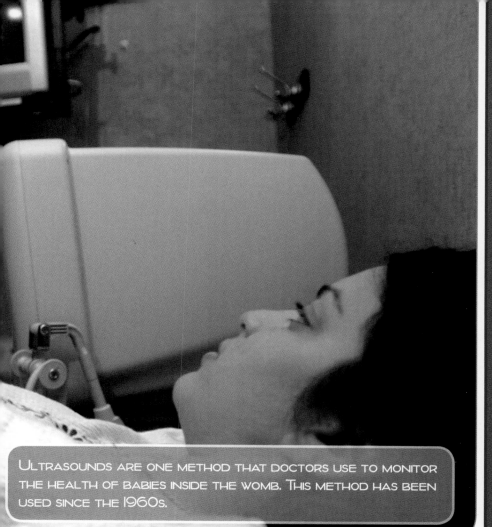

ULTRASOUNDS ARE ONE METHOD THAT DOCTORS USE TO MONITOR THE HEALTH OF BABIES INSIDE THE WOMB. THIS METHOD HAS BEEN USED SINCE THE 1960s.

During the pregnancy, doctors advise women to take prenatal vitamins, which contain higher levels of certain nutrients, such as folic acid. These nutrients aid the baby during growth, in addition to helping keep the mother healthy. Going on regular doctor visits, and taking vitamin supplements, eating a healthy diet, exercising regularly, and giving up smoking, drinking, and drugs are all important things a woman can do to have the healthiest pregnancy possible.

You've probably heard stories of women getting sick or having weird cravings during pregnancy. This is a fairly common occurrence, and pregnant women experience a variety of symptoms, including nausea or vomiting, heartburn, constipation, aches and pains in the abdomen and lower back, and tiredness. In the case of teen mothers, risks for both the mother and baby are heightened because:

- Teenage mothers are less likely to gain adequate weight during pregnancy, leading to low birth weight. Low birth weight is associated with several infant and childhood disorders and a higher rate of infant mortality. Babies with low birth weights are more likely to have organs that are not fully developed, which can result in complications, such as bleeding in the brain, respiratory distress syndrome, and intestinal problems.

- Teenage mothers have a higher rate of poor eating habits than older women and are less likely to take recommended daily prenatal multivitamins to maintain adequate nutrition during pregnancy. Teens are also more likely to smoke cigarettes, drink alcohol, or take drugs during pregnancy, which can cause health problems for the baby.

- Teenage mothers receive regular prenatal care less often than older women. According to the American Medical Association (AMA), babies born to women who do not have regular

♀ POSTPARTUM DEPRESSION

One of the more common mental side effects of pregnancy is postpartum depression. This usually occurs after the birth of the child and, according to the Mayo Clinic, affects an estimated 10 percent of new moms. Many new mothers experience some sadness and anxiety after having a child. But when these symptoms intensify and continue, it may be more than just a case of the blues. Signs of postpartum depression include:

- Loss of appetite
- Insomnia
- Intense irritability and anger
- Overwhelming fatigue
- Lack of joy in life
- Feelings of shame, guilt, or inadequacy
- Severe mood swings
- Difficulty bonding with the baby
- Withdrawal from family and friends
- Thoughts of harming yourself or the baby

prenatal care are four times more likely to die before the age of one year.

In addition to physical side effects, women can also experience a variety of mental and emotional side effects during and after pregnancy. Hormonal changes can cause emotions to change drastically from great happiness and excitement to sadness and depression.

There are a number of things that can contribute to postpartum depression. Physical changes like dramatic drops in the hormones estrogen and progestin can cause

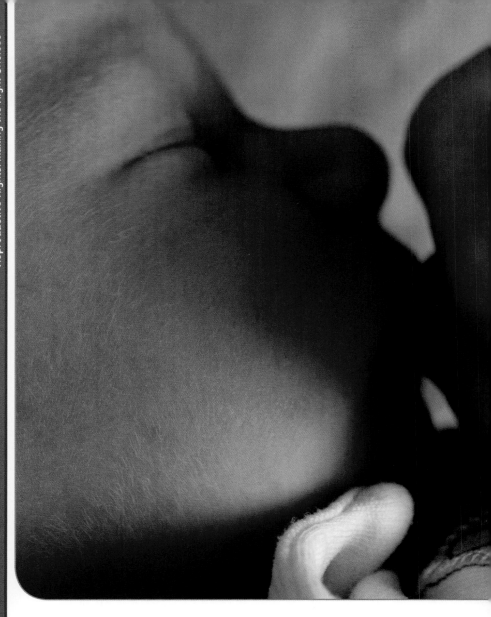

emotional changes. Being sleep deprived and overwhelmed with the care of an infant can leave new mothers feeling irritable and helpless. External factors like financial strains and lack of support from your partner or loved ones can

BECOMING A MOTHER IS ONE OF THE MOST REWARDING AND CHALLENGING THINGS A WOMAN CAN DO. BABIES REQUIRE A LOT OF CARE.

also lead to extra stress. Postpartum depression can be treated in a number of ways. Counseling, antidepressants, and hormone therapy are three of the most common methods of treating the condition.

ADOPTION

If you're pregnant and don't want to have an abortion, but you aren't ready to be a parent, there is another option—adoption. Adoption is a permanent legal agreement to allow someone else to raise your child. When trying to decide if adoption is the right choice for you, there are several questions to ask yourself:

- Am I ready to be a parent?
- Can I afford to be a parent now?
- What would it mean for my future if I had a child now?
- Can I accept not being my child's primary parent?
- Does adoption feel like what I should do, not what I want to do?
- Is someone pressuring me to choose adoption?
- Will I be able to cope with the feeling of loss that I may have?
- Do I have people in my life who will help me through the pregnancy and adoption process?
- How do I feel about other women who choose to place their children for adoption?
- How important is it to me what other people will think about my decision?

If you still think adoption is the best choice once you've answered those questions, the next step is exploring different types of adoption and how it all works.

There are two main types of adoption: open adoption and closed adoption. With an open adoption, the birth mother and adoptive parents work through the same contact. The mother selects the parents and can form a relationship with them. This type of adoption sometimes allows for a birth mother to get updates about the child, and possibly contact them, if it's agreed upon by both parties.

In closed, or confidential, adoptions, the birth mother and adopting parents do not know or have contact with each other. This type of adoption is becoming less common.

Adoptions are generally handled in one of three ways: agency adoption, independent adoption, or adoption by a relative. With an agency adoption, a state-licensed agency assists the birth mother with the process. It schedules pre-adoption and post-adoption counseling and often makes hospital arrangements. The agency helps the mother select adoptive parents, and it also can help with legal matters.

Independent adoptions are generally handled by a lawyer. It's important to choose your own lawyer in this case, and make sure you're comfortable with him or her.

With adoption by a relative, a member of the birth mother's family volunteers to adopt the child. The family members can work through a lawyer, adoption agency, or your state department of human services. Family adoptions must meet the same legal requirements of any other adoption. That means even if your child is placed with a family member, you have no more legal parental rights than if the child was placed with a stranger.

GIVING A CHILD UP FOR ADOPTION CAN BE A PAINFUL EXPERIENCE FOR MOTHERS. BUT WITH EFFORTS LIKE NATIONAL ADOPTION DAY, CHILDREN LIKE THE ONES IN THIS PHOTO CAN FIND LOVING HOMES.

Adoption laws are different in every state. If you decide this is the choice for you, seek help from an adoption counselor or agency to ensure your legal rights are protected throughout the process.

ABORTION

Abortion is a generally safe and common procedure that basically ends pregnancy. According to Planned Parenthood,

more than one in three women in the United States will have an abortion by the time they are forty-five years old. Women choose to have abortions for a variety of reasons. Some feel unprepared or too young or inexperienced to be a parent. Others aren't financially or emotionally ready for motherhood. If you're trying to decide if this major decision is right for you, there are several things to consider:

ABORTION IS A DIFFICULT DECISION THAT SHOULD BE SERIOUSLY CONSIDERED WITH THE HELP OF A PARENT OR OTHER TRUSTED ADULT.

- Am I ready to become a parent?
- Can I afford to have a child?
- Can I afford to have an abortion?
- What would it mean for my future and my family's future if I had a child now?
- Would I consider putting the child up for adoption instead?

- Do I have strong religious beliefs about abortion?
- How do I feel about other women having abortions?
- How important is it to me what other people will think about my decision?
- Can I handle the experience of having an abortion?

■ Is anyone pressuring me to have an abortion?

■ Am I being pressured not to have an abortion?

■ Would I be willing to tell a parent or go before a judge if my state requires it?

If you think abortion is the right choice for you, there are a couple of options after carefully considering these questions. An in-clinic abortion is a procedure that you go to a doctor or abortion provider's office to receive. This procedure is performed with medical instruments. The other type of abortion is the abortion pill, which a health care provider will give you at a clinic. You are then free to go home and will generally be prescribed antibiotics to take after the initial pill.

Women seeking abortions can find medical help, as well as counseling and other information, at women's health centers like Planned Parenthood. If there isn't a Planned Parenthood in your area, local health department clinics and even gynecologists can help provide any information and assistance that you may need.

Though it may be very scary, it's important for teens seeking abortion to talk to a parent or other adult they trust before making the decision. In some states, it's required for teens under the age of eighteen to notify a parent or guardian before obtaining an abortion. Even if this isn't the case in your state, you should still seek the help of an adult when making such an important choice.

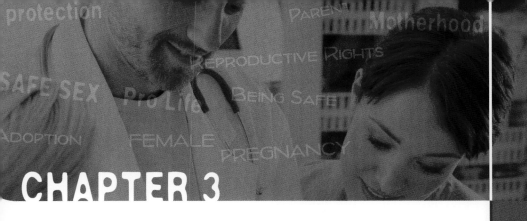

CHAPTER 3

A Brief History of Reproductive Rights

Y ou should feel lucky to become a woman at this point in history. Women today have more choices and rights than their ancestors could've ever dreamed of having. Less than a century ago, women in the United States couldn't even vote, much less make choices about other things in life, such as their reproductive rights.

Women of the past often didn't get much of a choice about their sexuality. Becoming a wife and mother was expected, and very few deviated from that norm. There were few ways to prevent or space pregnancies (the birth control pill was not available until the 1960s). Premarital sex was thought to be rare and definitely frowned-upon. And most women, as expected, married young, often before graduating or right out of high school.

This was especially true in pre-twentieth-century America. Many families worked on farms or in other family-owned businesses, and many saw having children as a necessity

In past centuries, the role of women was mostly limited to working within the home as a wife and mother.

to make sure there were enough hands ready to help. The role of women during this time was to be in the home, raising children, preparing meals, and tending to any other household chores. These women sometimes worked on the farm or business, but their primary role was as mother.

As the Industrial Revolution took off around the turn of the twentieth century, families began to move into cities, and roles began to change. More women began to take jobs outside the home, some working in the same factories that employed their husbands. This intensified during World War II, when women took over jobs their husbands left behind, and took over as heads of the house as well.

After having a taste of life outside the home, as well as control within the home, women's roles began to change. More women began putting off marriage to attend college. During these early years of what would eventually become the feminist and sexual revolution, women still had the fear of accidental pregnancy. Early condoms and other forms of birth control were rather unreliable, far more so than they are today. But then in 1960, a revolutionary invention was released that changed women's lives forever: the birth control pill.

During the 1950s, researchers began working on a pill that women could take to prevent pregnancy. It had been discovered during the 1930s that certain hormones would stop ovulation in rabbits, and scientists wanted to formulate something similar for humans. Women's rights advocate and Planned Parenthood founder, Margaret Sanger, helped underwrite research for the project, raising thousands of

♀ THE MOTHER OF THE REPRODUCTIVE RIGHTS MOVEMENT

Margaret Sanger was a troublemaker. At least that's what a lot of people thought when she opened the first birth control clinic in New York in 1916. She was promptly charged and convicted of "maintaining a public nuisance." But she appealed and won, opening the door for doctors to give birth control advice in New York City.

Sanger, who was born in 1883, began her career as a professional nurse in White Plains, New York. She worked with the poor in New York City, and, seeing their struggles firsthand, realized there was a great need for widespread information about contraception. So Sanger left her nursing career to promote birth control full-time. In 1914, she was indicted for circulating a magazine called *The Woman Rebel*, which attacked legislative restrictions on birth control. Two years later, she opened her birth control clinic in Brooklyn.

Shortly after, Sanger began publishing *Birth Control Review*, a monthly magazine that she edited until 1928. During the 1920s, she made history by forming the American Birth Control League, which later became Planned Parenthood. Working with this group, she founded the Birth Control Clinical Research Bureau in 1923 to promote birth control research and development.

Later in her life, Sanger served as honorary chairperson of Planned Parenthood and helped establish the International Planned Parenthood Federation in 1952. She served as its president until 1959. Sanger continued to work promoting birth control internationally for the rest of her life, traveling extensively in Asia and other areas. She died in 1966 in Tucson, Arizona.

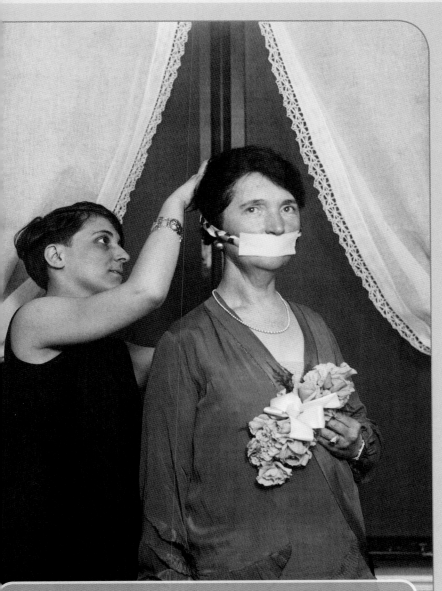

BIRTH CONTROL ADVOCATE MARGARET SANGER (SHOWN ABOVE WITH HER MOUTH COVERED) STAGED MANY PROTESTS, LIKE THE ONE PICTURED HERE, AGAINST THOSE WHO ATTEMPTED TO PREVENT WOMEN FROM OBTAINING BIRTH CONTROL.

dollars for the effort. In 1956, the first pill, Envoid, was created. It was approved for contraceptive use by the Food and Drug Administration in 1960.

So how did we get from that to where we are today? It was a lengthy process of changing social expectations,

differing economic times, and landmark court cases. One of the first of these cases was *Union Pacific Railway Co. v. Botsford* in 1891. The case was a civil suit filed by a female passenger that the railroad company attempted to force into having a physical examination after she was injured on the

DR. C. LEE BUXTON AND ESTELLE GRISWOLD *(SECOND FROM LEFT)* WERE PROSECUTED AFTER OPENING A BIRTH CONTROL CLINIC. EVENTUALLY, THE SUPREME COURT RULED IN THEIR FAVOR, LEGALIZING THE DISTRIBUTION OF BIRTH CONTROL TO MARRIED PEOPLE.

train. The Supreme Court rejected Union Pacific Railway's claim that they had a right to subject this woman to the examination, saying, "No right is held more sacred, or is more carefully guarded, by the common law, than the right of every individual to the possession and control of his own person, free from all restraint or interference of others." The court basically said we're all completely in charge of our own bodies, and have the right to control them.

One of the next major cases in the groundwork for reproductive rights is *Griswold v. Connecticut* in 1965. The case challenged a Connecticut law established in 1879 that prohibited the use of "any drug, medicinal article, or instrument for the purpose of preventing conception." Several previous cases challenged this law. The road to change didn't open until Estelle Griswold, then executive director of the Planned Parenthood League of Connecticut, and Dr. C. Lee Buxton, a physician and Yale professor, opened a birth control clinic in New Haven, Connecticut. Not long after they opened it, Griswold and Buxton were arrested, tried, found guilty, and fined $100 each. The decision was upheld by Connecticut courts and went all the way to the Supreme Court. In the end, the court ruled that on the basis of the constitutional right to privacy, married persons have the right to buy and use contraceptives.

A few years later, in 1971, *United States v. Vuitch* was the first case to challenge the ban on abortion in America. Washington, D.C., abortion provider Milan Vuitch was charged several times with providing abortions that the government deemed not necessary for the life or health of the woman, in accordance with the D.C. law. Vuitch challenged the law as being constitutionally vague in regard to the term "health." A district judge agreed and overturned his convictions. When it went to the Supreme Court, the court ruled that the term "health" was not vague, overturning the original ruling. While Vuitch ultimately lost, the decision began to change the idea of abortion, making it more of a question of a surgical procedure. The very next day, the court voted to hear *Roe v. Wade*.

ROE V. WADE: THE COURT DECISION AND ITS IMPACT

The *Roe v. Wade* case is one of the most well-known—if not the most well-known—court cases in American history. But while the verdict and the argument are common knowledge, the details of the case are a little cloudy in many minds. It all started in 1970, when Norma McCorvey, a pregnant woman from Dallas, Texas, challenged the state's abortion laws.

At the time, control over abortion legislation resided with the states, rather than the federal government. By the end of the nineteenth century, most states established statutes that made it a crime to perform or obtain an abortion, except to save the life of a pregnant woman. Most of these statutes were still in effect when McCorvey's case came up.

Using the alias "Jane Roe," McCorvey sued the Dallas County district attorney Henry Wade for the right to have an abortion. Her pregnancy did not threaten her life, but she was single and poor, and did not want to have a child she couldn't afford to raise. McCorvey and her attorneys asked the federal district court to rule that the Texas abortion statute violated her constitutional rights. They also asked the court to forbid the district attorney from prosecuting anyone else under the Texas abortion law in the future.

Surprisingly, the panel of judges ruled in favor of Roe on the grounds that the law violated her constitutional right to privacy. However, the court refused to forbid future prosecutions for abortion, so McCorvey and her attorneys appealed to the Supreme Court. Wade also appealed the decision.

The Supreme Court heard arguments in the case in 1971. After intense debate among the justices, Chief Justice Warren Berger recommended the case be reargued, as he did not find it as black and white as some of the other justices. Both sides came back in the fall of 1972 to reargue. After presenting their cases, the Court decided

NORMA MCCORVEY, AKA "JANE ROE," TOOK HER CASE TO THE SUPREME COURT, WHICH RULED IN HER FAVOR, LEGALIZING THE PRACTICE OF ABORTION.

7–2 in favor of McCorvey (Roe) in January 1973. Justice Harry A. Blackmun wrote the Court's majority opinion, stating that while there were certainly moral and religious considerations concerning abortion, the case had to be decided on the basis of constitutional rights.

As you know, this was a huge moment for those fighting for, and against, abortion. *Roe v. Wade* effectively legalized abortion in the United States, ruling most state bans as unconstitutional. The decision served as a legal precedent for at least twenty more Supreme Court cases. It opened the door for women to receive safe, accessible

THE PASSING OF *ROE V. WADE* IGNITED BOTH THE PRO-CHOICE AND ANTIABORTION MOVEMENTS IN THE UNITED STATES. IT IS STILL CONTROVERSIAL TODAY.

abortion services. In 1965, 17 percent of all pregnancy- and childbirth-related deaths resulted from illegal abortion. Today, abortions are eleven times safer than they were then.

The right to make decisions about whether or not to have children changed women's lives in other ways as well. It enabled young women to pursue educational and employment opportunities that were unthinkable to those of previous generations. Even the Supreme Court noted in 1992: "The ability of women to participate equally in the economic and social life of the nation has been facilitated by their ability to control their reproductive lives."

THE POST-ROE V. WADE WORLD: THE BIRTH OF THE PRO-CHOICE V. PRO-LIFE DEBATE

Not everyone was thrilled with the *Roe v. Wade* decision. Many people found it morally and ethically wrong. In 1973, a group of those opposed to the ruling gathered in Detroit, Michigan. This was the beginning of the National Right to Life Committee (NRLC). According to their mission statement, their ultimate goal was to "restore legal protection to innocent human life."

Since that first gathering, the organization has grown to more than three thousand chapters in all fifty states. They've become a powerful lobbying presence in Washington, helping pass a number of legislative reforms. While their main cause is the opposition of abortion, they don't have an official stance on other reproductive rights issues like contraception and sex education.

After the NRLC, many other pro-life groups formed. In response to that, the pro-choice movement evolved.

Planned Parenthood is one of the major groups in this movement, joined by NARAL (National Abortion and Reproductive Rights Action League) Pro-Choice America, the Center for Reproductive Rights, and the National Organization for Women (NOW). These groups work to oppose pretty much everything the pro-life groups work for, both in the courts and on a grassroots level.

Those fights in the courts began shortly after *Roe v. Wade* and have continued until the present day. A big win for the pro-choice movement came in 1976 with *Planned Parenthood v. Danforth*. In the 6–3 ruling, the Court struck down a requirement for married women to get their husband's permission to get an abortion. In the same decision, the Court voted down a statute requiring minors seeking abortions to obtain the written consent of a parent. Both decisions were made on the basis that these statutes granted an unconstitutional veto power to a third party. These rulings were another big win for the pro-choice movement.

Just a few months later, in September 1976, Congress enacted the first Hyde Amendment, so named because of its sponsor, Representative Henry Hyde of Illinois. The amendment prohibited federal funding for abortions through Medicaid and all other Health and Human Services programs. The original measure made no exception in cases of rape, incest, or when pregnancy threatened the woman's life. Public outcry from reproductive rights groups led to the addition of language in 1977 making exceptions for these cases. Today, however, the

Hyde Amendment does not include exceptions for when the pregnancy threatens a woman's health. The passing of the amendment was a major win for the pro-life movement. The debate over it continues to this day, with abortion rights advocates arguing that federal Medicaid funds should cover abortion, just as they cover pregnancy and childbirth costs.

The debate on abortion goes on. But the strides made in the advancement of reproductive rights for women would surely surprise the women of generations past.

CHAPTER 4

THE PRO-LIFE MOVEMENT

Not everyone thinks the *Roe v. Wade* decision, and abortion in general, are a good thing. You may not agree with the legalization of abortion yourself. There's nothing wrong with that. Part of reproductive rights is having the right to choose, and that means you can choose not to agree with abortion. There are many individuals and groups in this country that oppose abortion for a variety of reasons.

One of the main reasons people oppose abortion is because of their moral or religious objections to the practice. They believe that life begins when a child is conceived. So aborting a fetus is the same as murder, which is forbidden by the Bible. Many faiths and denominations hold this belief, and the Catholic Church in particular maintains that abortion is a grave sin.

Another objection to abortion is based on physical risks associated with the procedure. While abortion is one of the most common and safest surgical procedures in the United States, it is still a surgical procedure. Some of the

risks associated with surgical procedures include infection, scarring, and injury due to doctor error. For some who oppose abortion, the possibility of injuring the reproductive organs, or overall health of a woman, is another reason they're against the procedure.

The negative mental and emotional effects sometimes associated with abortion is another reason some oppose it.

PEOPLE OPPOSE ABORTION FOR A NUMBER OF REASONS. SOME ARE OPPOSED BECAUSE OF RELIGIOUS BELIEFS THAT THEY SAY PROHIBIT THE PROCEDURE.

Many women feel a range of emotions after having an abortion. These emotions can include anger, regret, guilt, or sadness, and they can be quite strong. For many, these emotions fade over time. But for others, they can last a very long time. Some women can feel serious depression or experience other emotional problems after an abortion. For some, having an abortion can be a significant life event,

like ending a relationship, starting or losing a job, or becoming a parent. It can be very stressful and difficult. The American Psychiatric Association has determined that the risks of experiencing mental health problems after an abortion are the same as carrying an unplanned pregnancy to term and giving birth.

STUDENTS FOR LIFE, A COLLEGE-BASED PRO-LIFE GROUP, STAGES PROTESTS ON CAMPUSES ACROSS THE NATION. PEOPLE OF ALL AGES TAKE PART.

LEADERS IN THE PRO-LIFE MOVEMENT

Just as in the pro-choice movement, there are a number of groups and individuals leading the antiabortion cause. These people and groups agree with the objections stated previously, and they're committed to fighting abortion and eventually overturning the *Roe v. Wade* decision. You may have seen extreme antiabortion protesters on the news, but the people who commit crimes and attack abortion providers are not representative of most in the pro-life movement. Most pro-life groups work within the system, lobbying politicians and attempting to help pass legislation that restricts abortion. They also hold protests and produce publications to get their message out to the general public.

One of the leading groups in the pro-life movement is the National Right to Life Committee (NRLC). As we mentioned in the last chapter, the group formed shortly after the *Roe v. Wade* decision, and today they're the leading group working against abortion. The group lobbies state and federal governments to pass antiabortion legislation. They also keep tallies of where politicians stand on the issue and how they vote.

An offshoot of the NRLC is National College Students for Life. This is a pro-life organization for college-age students, run by students. According to their Web site, the group's mission includes "educating our college communities about the value of human life, instilling respect for the individual lives of all people, and creating a society that will offer life-affirming solutions to the tragedies of abortion, infanticide, and euthanasia." Since they work on the college level, their efforts mostly include influencing young voters and changing individual minds about the abortion issue.

EVEN THOUGH MOST PEOPLE ASSUME ALL DEMOCRATS ARE PRO-CHOICE, THAT'S NOT THE CASE. DEMOCRATS FOR LIFE REPRESENTS MEMBERS OF THE POLITICAL PARTY OPPOSED TO ABORTION.

Another group affiliated with the NRLC is Hispanic Americans for Life. Their mission is the same as the NRLC, except their focus is within the Hispanic American community. Due to the fact that many of Hispanic descent are Catholics, this means many within the community oppose abortion based on their religious beliefs.

Aside from the abortion issue, many pro-life groups, especially religious-based ones, advocate abstinence-only sex education for youth. This means they don't want your school or teachers talking to you about birth control options, other than abstaining from sex. This abstinence-only stance also limits access to contraceptives for students. The philosophy of abstinence-only education is based on the religious belief that premarital sex is a sin, and no one—especially teens—should engage in sex before marriage.

Pro-life Legislation

One of the main objectives of the pro-life movement is to overturn *Roe v. Wade*, banning abortion in the United States. They hope to achieve this goal through changes to both federal and state legislation.

In 2006, South Dakota enacted a near-ban on abortion within the state, but it was rejected by the state's voters that year. The state again put the initiative on the ballot in 2008. Again, it was voted down by citizens. Attempts to pass state bans like this is one of the ways that antiabortion groups work to challenge the *Roe v. Wade* ruling. Twelve states considered near-bans on abortion in 2008.

Antiabortion groups celebrated a big victory in 2007 when the Supreme Court voted 5–4 in the case *Gonzales*

MISCONCEPTIONS ABOUT THE PRO-LIFE MOVEMENT

One of the major misconceptions about the pro-life movement is that all its members are radicals. These radical protesters, the people who commit criminal acts and violence, are among the fringe of the movement and are condemned by most mainstream antiabortion groups. While some of the more mainstream groups still stage protests, they are usually nonviolent protests.

Another misconception is that the abortion issue is clearly divided politically. Generally, most members of the Republican Party oppose abortion, while most Democrats support a woman's right to choose. However, there are differing opinions on both sides. Some Republicans, such as members of the Republican Majority for Choice (an organization of pro-choice Republicans), support abortion rights. And some Democrats, such as those in the group Democrats for Life (a pro-life group for Democrats), oppose abortion rights.

v. *Carhart* to uphold the federal abortion ban passed by Congress and signed by President George W. Bush in 2003. The ban criminalizes a particular form of abortion, referred to as partial-birth abortion. Many doctors say this is the safest type of procedure and the best to protect the woman's health. The term "partial-birth" is not a medical term though. It was coined in 1995 by the antiabortion movement to categorize abortions performed after the twentieth week of pregnancy through the dilation and extraction or, D&X, method. This procedure involves removing the fetus intact by dilating a pregnant woman's cervix, then pulling the entire body out through the birth

Long before birth...
toes and fingers wiggle,
and hearts beat

CHOOSE LIFE

canal. Groups like the NRLC work hard to ban this procedure.

The ban also broke from previous rulings on abortion-related cases by declaring that the ban is constitutional, even though it does not have an exception for when the woman's health is at risk.

AS LONG AS ABORTION REMAINS LEGAL, THE ANTIABORTION MOVEMENT WILL CONTINUE TO WORK TO CHANGE THE LAW.

Obviously, the issue of abortion is a very complicated one. And the two opposing sides will continue to work against each other, since with every win for one, the other experiences a loss.

Myths and Facts

Myth

Emergency contraception (the morning after pill) is the same thing as having an abortion.

Fact

The hormones that are in the morning after pill work by keeping a woman's ovaries from releasing eggs (ovulation). Pregnancy cannot happen if there is no egg to join with sperm. The hormones in the morning after pill also prevent pregnancy by thickening a woman's cervical mucus. The mucus blocks sperm and keeps it from joining with an egg. It does not abort fetuses or fertilized eggs.

Myth

You can tell if a person has an STD.

Fact

Many STDs, such as chlamydia and gonorrhea, do not have noticeable symptoms. Even HIV's symptoms often don't show up for years after infection. So a person might have an STD and not even know it. And if they don't know, you certainly can't tell just by looking at them.

MYTH

You can't get pregnant the first time you have sex.

Fact

You can get pregnant any time you have unprotected sex, be it the first or one hundredth time. If sperm reaches one of your eggs, it doesn't matter whether you've had sex before or not. You can get pregnant. You can even become pregnant before you have your first period, since ovulation occurs about fourteen days before your period appears. So you could be ovulating for the first time and not know it until two weeks later.

CHAPTER 5

THE PRO-CHOICE MOVEMENT

For pro-choice groups, every victory for the pro-life movement is a new obstacle to overcome. While abortion is legal, that right is constantly under attack. Other freedoms, such as access to affordable health care and birth control, are not guaranteed. During the presidency of George W. Bush, the pro-choice movement weathered several blows to their cause with legislation both at the state and federal levels. There was the ban on partial-birth abortions signed in 2003, which was upheld by the Supreme Court with the help of pro-life Justices Roberts and Alito in 2007. In 2006, the House of Representatives passed the Child Interstate Abortion Notification Act, also known as the "Teen Endangerment Act." This act would have restricted the ability of teens to receive abortions outside their home state, whether or not the abortions are to protect the teens' health. It was not signed into law, and the next Congress did not vote on it.

Supreme Court justice Samuel Alito (*left*) and Chief Justice John Roberts (*right*) are both conservative judges who oppose abortion.

In addition to these laws, proposals and statutes have been introduced that attempt to restrict reproductive rights. One such proposal concerns parental consent for teens to obtain contraceptives. Currently, there are no laws that require teens to get their parents' permission to get birth control. Two federal programs—Title X , which funds low-cost family planning, and Medicaid, which helps low-income individuals get health care—protect teens' privacy and prohibit parental consent requirements. But there are several groups, as well as politicians, who are working to change. Throughout state capitals and in Congress, legislators continue to focus on hundreds of bills relating to reproductive rights.

LEADERS IN REPRODUCTIVE RIGHTS ACTIVISM

Planned Parenthood is not the only organization in the fight for reproductive rights. There are many other groups and individuals, too. These groups fight for a number of issues, including accessible health care for women, availability of birth control, adequate sex education for adolescents, and abortion rights.

One of the leaders in reproductive rights advocacy is NARAL Pro-Choice America. This nonprofit group has fought the battle for women's reproductive rights for more than thirty years. Their mission, to protect women's right to privacy and right to choose, is carried out through a number of ways. At the legislative level, they lobby Congress to fight bills that threaten abortion rights. On a

NARAL Pro-Choice America is one of the leading groups in the pro-choice movement. The group stages protests and lobbies Congress to uphold *Roe v. Wade*.

more grassroots level, they work to get pro-choice candidates elected through organizing and informing voters across the country. They also conduct continuous research and analysis of legislative bills and the actions of politicians in order to keep their supporters informed.

Another prominent group is the Center for Reproductive Rights. This nonprofit legal advocacy organization is dedicated to promoting and defending women's reproductive rights worldwide. The group was founded in 1992 as the Center for Reproductive Law and Policy, contributing to two significant reproductive rights cases: *Stenberg v. Carhart* in 2000 and *Ferguson v. City of Charleston* in 2001. The group works within the law to achieve their goals: promoting access to contraception, ensuring access to abortion, supporting adolescent reproductive health care, guaranteeing reproductive freedom for low-income women, and countering violence against women's reproductive freedom. The center uses its legal resources—lawyers, researchers, and other legal professionals—to fight for these goals in courts in the United States and abroad.

The National Organization for Women (NOW) doesn't solely work to promote and protect reproductive rights, but it's one of their main objectives. Founded in 1966 by a small group of women's rights activists, NOW has more than half a million members across the nation. They work to give and maintain equal rights for women in all arenas. In their efforts to advance reproductive freedom for women, they stage protests, educate the public and media, lobby lawmakers, and assist in court cases.

♀ THE ACLU

The American Civil Liberties Union (ACLU) isn't simply a reproductive rights group. In fact, they're not even solely a women's rights group. The ACLU fights for the liberties of all citizens, particularly those related to the right of free speech, right to equal protection under the law, right to due process, and right to privacy. This last right is where the ACLU's role in the reproductive rights movement comes in. Under the constitutional right to privacy, women can have abortions, get birth control, and have control over their own bodies. The ACLU advocates for these rights in Congress and state legislatures, and in the courts with lawyers across the nation.

While these are some of the most prominent groups, there are hundreds of others on the local and regional levels working hard every day to protect women's reproductive rights. With the help of thousands of workers and volunteers, they take on the courts and politicians in this country to ensure that women maintain their rights.

WHAT'S NEXT? THE FUTURE OF REPRODUCTIVE RIGHTS

The struggle for reproductive rights is an ongoing, evolving one. From new legislation to birth control innovations, there's always something happening that can possibly affect the lives of women.

Doctors and researchers are constantly working to create better methods of birth control with higher rates of effectiveness and fewer side effects. New innovations, such as the current IUDs on the market, give women new freedom because they're so easy and effective. With the HPV vaccine that helps prevent the risk of cervical cancer, these medical advances can also save lives.

THE ELECTION OF BARACK OBAMA WAS A MAJOR VICTORY FOR THE PRO-CHOICE MOVEMENT. THE NEW PRESIDENT HAS PLEDGED TO UPHOLD THE *ROE V. WADE* DECISION AND HAS OVERTURNED SOME OF PRESIDENT BUSH'S ANTIABORTION MANDATES.

In addition to new inventions and medical advancements, the increased availability of sexual education and birth control for adolescents is one of the most positive effects of the reproductive rights movement. Allowing young women to be informed about their sexuality, and the risks associated with it, helps them make informed choices. When you know all the risks and options, it makes that important choice of whether or not to have sex easier to make.

With the election of Barack Obama in 2008, the reproductive rights movement celebrated a great victory. Obama is a pro-choice president, and he filled his cabinet with other pro-choice leaders, such as Secretary of State Hillary Clinton and Vice President Joe Biden. This was an especially big win for pro-choice advocates because many believe the balance of the Supreme Court will change during the next four to eight years with the possible retirement of several elder justices. With former president Bush's appointments of two conservative justices, many pro-choice groups were concerned that the election of a conservative president would mean more conservative justices in the court. If these justices gained a majority, the *Roe v. Wade* decision could possibly be overturned.

So the election of Obama was a major one. In the first week of his presidency, Obama reversed a global ban enacted by the Bush administration on giving federal money to international groups that perform abortions or provide abortion information.

But one of the most important factors in the future of reproductive rights is young women like you. You are the future of our nation. By keeping yourself informed and involved in maintaining your rights and beliefs, whatever those beliefs may be, you ensure that future generations will enjoy the same freedoms that you do.

abortion Termination of pregnancy.

abstinence Not having sex; a birth control method.

AIDS Acquired immunodeficiency syndrome; a terminal sexually transmitted disease that weakens the immune system to the point that the body can no longer fight off infection.

bacterial vaginosis A common bacterial infection of the vagina.

birth control patch A birth control method that uses an adhesive patch, attached to the skin, to release hormones into the body to prevent pregnancy.

birth control pill One of the oldest methods of birth control, the pill contains hormones that prevent pregnancy.

birth control shot An injection of hormones used to prevent pregnancy.

birth control vaginal ring A small plastic ring inserted into the vagina to prevent pregnancy by releasing hormones into the body.

cervical cap A small silicone cup that covers the cervix to prevent pregnancy.

cervix The lower narrow part of the uterus that opens into the vaginal canal.

chlamydia A common bacterial sexually transmitted disease that often goes untreated because it has little to no symptoms.

condom A latex or plastic sheath used to cover the penis during sex to prevent pregnancy and disease.

contraceptive An agent or device used to prevent pregnancy; also known as birth control.

diaphragm A shallow, dome-shaped cup made of latex that covers the cervix to prevent pregnancy.

emergency contraception A pill that can be taken up to five days after unprotected sex to prevent pregnancy.

female condom A plastic pouch inserted into the vagina to prevent pregnancy.

genital herpes A sexually transmitted disease caused by the herpes simplex virus type 2; it causes blisters on the genitals and cannot be cured.

genital HPV A viral sexually transmitted infection that affects the skin and mucous membranes of the genital area; the disease sometimes produces warts and can make women more susceptible to cervical cancer.

gonorrhea A common bacterial sexually transmitted disease that often goes untreated because it has little to no symptoms.

HIV Human immunodeficiency virus, the sexually transmitted virus that causes AIDS.

IUD Short for intrauterine device, an IUD is a small plastic device inserted into the uterus by a health professional to prevent pregnancy.

LGV Lymphogranuloma venereum is a bacterial sexually transmitted disease that can cause bumps or ulcers on the genitals.

PID Pelvic inflammatory disease, or PID, is an infection of the uterus, fallopian tubes, and other reproductive organs that can lead to infertility; a common complication of STDs like gonorrhea and chlamydia.

postpartum depression Depression that occurs after giving birth, often caused by stress, hormonal changes, and lack of sleep, among other things.

pro-choice movement The political and social movement that advocates a woman's right to choose whether or not to have a child; advocates the legalization of abortion and accessibility to birth control and sex education.

pro-life movement The political and social movement that opposes abortion, some methods of birth control, and, in some cases, sex education in schools.

Roe v. Wade The Supreme Court case that legalized abortion in 1976.

sterilization Closing or blocking of a woman's fallopian tubes to permanently prevent pregnancy.

syphilis A bacterial sexually transmitted disease that has symptoms often mistaken for other diseases.

trichomoniasis A common sexually transmitted disease caused by the single-celled protozoan parasite *Trichomonas vaginalis*.

withdrawal method A method of birth control where a man pulls his penis out of the vagina before ejaculation.

Abortion Rights Coalition of Canada

P.O. Box 2663, Station Main

Vancouver, BC V6B 3W3

Canada

(888) 642-2725

Web site: http://www.arcc-cdac.ca

The Abortion Rights Coalition of Canada's mission is to ensure women's reproductive freedom by protecting and advancing access to abortion and quality reproductive health care.

Democrats for Life of America

601 Pennsylvania Avenue NW

South Building, Suite 900

Washington, DC 2004

(202) 220-3066

Web site: http://www.democratsforlife.org

Democrats for Life of America is a national organization for pro-life members of the Democratic Party.

National Abortion Federation

1660 L Street NW, Suite 450

Washington, DC 20036

(202) 667-5881

(800) 772-9100 (hotline)

Web site: http://www.prochoice.org

This is a professional association of abortion providers in North America. It works to support health care workers who provide the right of reproductive choice.

NAF Canada

P.O. Box 42065
Victoria, BC V8R 1T2
Canada
(250) 598-1858
Web site: http://www.prochoice.org/canada/
NAF_canada.html

The National Abortion Federation (NAF) is the professional association of abortion providers in the United States and Canada. It believes that women should be trusted to make private medical decisions in consultation with their health care providers.

National Organization for Women

1100 H Street NW, 3rd floor
Washington, DC 20005
(202) 628-8669
Web site: http://www.now.org

The National Organization for Women (NOW) is an advocacy group that works for equal rights for women.

National Women's Health Information Center

U.S. Department of Health and Human Services
8270 Willow Oaks Corporate Drive
Fairfax, VA 22031
(800) 994-9662
Web site: http://www.4woman.gov

The Office on Women's Health was established in 1991 within the U.S. Department of Health and Human Services. Its vision is to ensure that "all women and girls are healthier and have a better sense of well-being by providing leadership to promote health equity for women and girls through sex/gender-specific approaches."

National Women's Health Resource Center

157 Broad Street, Suite 106
Red Bank, NJ 07701
(877) 986-9472
Web site: http://www.healthywomen.org
The National Women's Health Resource Center provides in-depth, objective, physician-approved information on a broad range of women's health issues.

WEB SITES

Due to the changing nature of Internet links, Rosen Publishing has developed an online list of Web sites related to the subject of this book. This site is updated regularly. Please use this link to access the list:

http://www.rosenlinks.com/wom/repr

Armstrong, Nancy, and Henderson, Elizabeth. *100 Questions You'd Never Ask Your Parents*. Richmond, VA: Uppman Publishing, 2007.

Balkin, Jack. *What* Roe v. Wade *Should Have Said: The Nation's Top Legal Experts Rewrite America's Most Controversial Decision*. New York, NY: New York University Press, 2007.

Baumgardner, Jennifer. *Abortion & Life*. New York, NY: Akashic Books, 2008.

Corinna, Heather. *S.E.X: The All-You-Need-to-Know Progressive Sexuality Guide to Get You Through High School and College*. Cambridge, MA: Da Capo Press, 2007.

Ehrenreich, Nancy. *The Reproductive Rights Reader: Law, Medicine and the Construction of Motherhood*. New York, NY: New York University Press, 2008.

Ehrlich, J. Shoshanna. *Who Decides? The Abortion Rights of Teens*. Westport, CT: Praeger Publishers, 2006.

Guddat, Gina. *Unwrapped: Real Questions Asked by Real Girls (About Sex)*. Houston, TX: Providence Publishing Corporation, 2007.

Sanger, Margaret. *The Autobiography of Margaret Sanger*. Mineola, NY: Dover Publications, 2004.

American Civil Liberties Union. "About Us." Retrieved December 21, 2008 (http://www.aclu.org/about).

Center for Reproductive Rights. "Parental Consent and Notice for Contraceptives Threatens Teen Health and Constitutional Rights." Retrieved December 21, 2008 (http://www.reproderechos.org/pub_fac_parentalconsent.html).

Center for Reproductive Rights. "Privacy Law and the U.S. Supreme Court: Before and After *Roe v. Wade.*" Retrieved December 21, 2008 (http://reproductiverights.org/document/privacy-law-and-the-us-supreme-court-before-and-after-roe-v-wade).

Center for Reproductive Rights. "The Teen Endangerment Act." Retrieved December 21, 2009 (http://reproductiverights.org/en/document/the-teen-endangerment-act-hr-748-s8396403-harming-young-women-who-seek-abortions).

Centers for Disease Control and Prevention. "STDs." Retrieved December 21, 2008 (http://www.cdc.gov/std/default.htm).

Chesler, Ellen. *Woman of Valor: Margaret Sanger and the Birth Control Movement in America.* New York, NY: Simon & Schuster, 2007.

40 Days for Life. "Campaign." Retrieved January 8, 2009. (http://www.40daysforlife.com/about.cfm?selected=campaign).

NARAL Pro-Choice America. "The Federal Abortion Ban." Retrieved December 21, 2008 (http://www. prochoiceamerica.org/issues/abortion/abortion-bans/ federal-abortion-ban.html).

National Organization for Women. "Advancing Reproductive Freedom." Retrieved December 21, 2008 (http://www.now.org/issues/abortion/index.html).

National Right to Life. "Mission Statement." Retrieved January 8, 2009 (http://www.nrlc.org/ Missionstatement.htm).

Planned Parenthood. "Birth Control Methods." Retrieved December 21, 2008 (http://www.plannedparenthood. org/health-topics/birth-control-4211.htm).

Planned Parenthood Affiliates of California. "Roe v. Wade: Its History and Impact." Retrieved December 21, 2008 (http://www.ppacca.org/site/pp.asp?c=kuJYJeO4F& b=139531).

Rovner, Julie. "Partial-Birth Abortion: Separating Fact from Spin." NPR.com. Retrieved December 30, 2008 (http://www.npr.org/templates/story/story.php? storyId=5168163).

U.S. Supreme Court. Roe v. Wade. Charleston, SC: BiblioBazaar, 2007.

Women's Health Channel. "Teen Pregnancy." Retrieved January 8, 2009 (http://www.womenshealthchannel. com/teenpregnancy/index.shtml).

ABOUT THE AUTHOR

Jennifer Bringle has always been fascinated with the issue of reproductive rights, especially since it so personally affects her life as a woman. She's written for a number of publications and also writes nonfiction books for teens.

PHOTO CREDITS

Designer: Nicole Russo; Editor: Bethany Bryan;
Photo Researcher: Amy Feinberg

LONGWOOD PUBLIC LIBRARY
800 Middle Country Road
Middle Island, NY 11953
(631) 924-6400
mylpl.net

LIBRARY HOURS

Monday-Friday	9:30 a.m. - 9:00 p.m.
Saturday	9:30 a.m. - 5:00 p.m.
Sunday (Sept-June)	1:00 p.m. - 5:00 p.m.